New Mills History Note

THE NEW MILLS AIR RAID
FRIDAY 3RD JULY 1942

by
Derek Brumhead

New Mills Local History Society

1990

Published by New Mills Local History Society
Editor, Ron Weston, The Thorns, Laneside Road,
New Mills, via Stockport, SK12 4LU

First published 1990

ISBN 0 9515926 1 0

ACKNOWLEDGEMENTS

Some of the material in this book was first published in my article in the "Courier Independent" of October 1988 (Now the "High Peak Courier".) Thanks are due to that paper for the sketch of the JU 88(A4) on the front cover and the idea for the map. I should also like to thank : Mr John Duckworth, Mr Harold Greenwood, the Rev. Maurice Handford, and Mrs Fanny Larkum (on behalf of her late husband) for the use of the eye witness accounts: Ron Collier for the information on the fate of the two German aircraft and the use of his photograph of one of those aircraft: and the New Mills Town Council for the use of their files on the air raid.

Cover illustration: Ju88 (A4) from an original by
Roni

THE NEW MILLS AIR RAID, FRIDAY 3 JULY 1942

INTRODUCTION

During the big blitzes on Manchester in the early part of the 1939-45 war, the hills around New Mills were lit up with flashes, the red glow of huge fires, and the pencil beams of searchlights. Enemy aircraft droned overhead but the Peak District escaped deliberate attack although random bombs were dropped particularly as the German pilots headed for home. As the war progressed, the sustained attacks on towns and cities grew less and the Germans resorted often to hit and run raids. It was one of these on Friday 3 July 1942 that brought the war physically to New Mills.

At 8.00pm - the Town Hall clock was actually striking the hour - when many people were watching a Will Hay film in the Union Road Cinema, two German aircraft,twin-engined JU 88s (Type A4), approached New Mills from a south-westerly direction up the Goyt valley. They appear to have split up slightly, one following the direction of the main railway viaduct line where it dropped two bombs in Woodside Street.The other aircraft banked over the gasholder in Mousley Bottom where it dropped a bomb and machine gunned the streets and cricket field, where a number of children were assembled. The aircraft continued to Low Leighton where another bomb was dropped, demolishing two houses and the Methodist Chapel, killing two people. A number of incendiary bombs were also dropped. From here the aircraft proceeded to Hayfield where another bomb caused more serious damage and deaths. No Air Raid Warning was received in the town. Both aircraft were later shot down over Lincolnshire.

A Town Hall note book records that there were 150 reports of damage to property in the town. By December 1942, the Council had paid out £727 to contractors for repairs mainly for broken windows and frames, doors, hinges and locks,fallen plaster on walls and ceilings, roofs and slates,gutters, and bullet holes. In addition, two semi-detached stone houses and the Methodist Chapel were demolished at Low Leighton.The Area Organiser reported that in New Mills, two people were killed and ten injured.

WOODSIDE STREET

Two bombs were dropped in Woodside Street,one failing to explode. It was reported that one bomb in its flight went first through the window of the Labour Exchange before embedding itself in the railway embankment.The unexploded bomb was found to be ripped open and the detonator exposed, although damaged. The Chief Warden gave instructions for this to be removed and it was taken to the Police Station.There was one casualty arising from this incident,who suffered from shock but refused to go to hospital.

MOUSLEY BOTTOM

The other aircraft banked over Mousley Bottom and dropped two bombs. One narrowly missed the Gas Holder at Mousley Bottom shedding its fins on the way and exploded in the bed of the river causing extensive damage to Lowe's mill, where all the windows and in many cases the window frames were blown out. There was also extensive damage to houses and windows in Union Road and Market Street.

At the same time, machine gun fire penetrated the Gasholder and Purifiers and small fires were started. These were dealt with by the Gas Works staff and the National Fire Service who had been called out by hand, the telephone being out of order.The Gas Works staff dealt with a potentially serious situation,and succeeded in patching up the holes and the supply was not interrupted.

Two tail fins of bombs were found, one on the ground and one embedded. The unexploded bomb was found in the river bed, and a large portion of its case had been torn away exposing the fuse and charge.The Area Organiser reported that when he arrived he found that

4

the bomb had been removed in a wheelbarrow from the
bed of the river by mill workmen and deposited on a
bank some 25 feet high "thus exposing mill to greater
damage should the bomb detonate".This incident was to
result in 13 men being prosecuted later and bound over
for twelve months in the sum of £5.

It was also reported that a large number of incendiary
bombs were also released, but no fires started and a
very large number of the devices failed to ignite.
Considerable damage was done by the machine gun fire
but there were no casualties. A large hole which can
still be seen in the railway fence about halfway down
Station Road (opposite house No 2) is reputed to have
been caused by a German bullet.Some streets and the
cricket field where a number of children were playing
were also machine gunned but fortunately there were no
casualties here.

LOW LEIGHTON

The aircraft continued to Low Leighton where a bomb
demolished two stone semi-detached houses, Whitfield
Villas (occupied by Mr and Mrs Handford and Mr and Mrs
Travis) and the "tin" Methodist Chapel(also referred to
as the Mission Hall).Incendiary bombs were also
dropped, many of which did not explode; five were
handed in later to the Low Leighton Smithy . Extensive
damage was done to the roofs and windows of the
"Public Assistance Institute" (now Ollersett View
Hospital)and surrounding houses.There was also more
machine gun fire.

In this attack, Joan Handford ten years of age, was
killed in one of the houses. Five other persons were
wounded, one of whom, Mr Dan McKellar died the next day
in hospital in Glossop as a result of being struck by
bullets and falling debris.The girl's brother, Maurice,
who was then 18,was rescued from the wreckage of his
home. (He has recently left Trinity Church, Buxton,
where he was incumbent for twenty years).Both his
parents were out of the house at the time.Also rescued
was Mrs Gillies, aged 75, the mother-in-law of Mr

Handford. A cat and dog were also recovered from the wrecked houses. By a fortunate chance Mr and Mrs Travis and their twins were also ,unusually,out at the time.Two other persons were injured in this incident .The houses were rebuilt soon after the end of the war in practically the same style. A new Methodist Church was built in the late 1950s in High Hill Road.The graves of Joan Handford and Daniel McKellar can be seen in St George's Churchyard.They are inscribed "Killed by enemy action".

From Low Leighton, the two aircraft proceeded to Hayfield where further bombing caused damage and fatal casualties.No Air Raid Warning was received in the town.

EYE WITNESS ACCOUNTS

1. Transcript of part of a recorded talk made in July 1987 by Mr W Greenwood of 31 New Street.

"It was a Friday evening... I used to go down to the Liberal Club to play snooker... Just as I was going up the steps, Wilf Mort who worked at Woodford those days was stood there... He said 'look, a plane's coming there and it's misfiring badly'... As we watched it approach...it came right over the Union Road Bridge... and I could see the pilot and either the observer or co-pilot sat next to him in the forward seat and it was only about 15-20 feet above the bridge and it went towards what we call Gowhole up the valley... then it circled round and swung round and as it went over the horizon approximately to Kinderscout as we call it there was a puff of brown-black smoke and Wilf said 'he's crashed ! Come on.' And he had his car... and of course we went into Low Leighton. Well,of course, when we got opposite the Workhouse we could see the tin chapel had gone and also the houses. We were the first on scene actually and there was a woman lay under the wall and a fragment had hit her on the thigh here and we picked her up and while we were doing all this Dr Millward came and he was the first Doctor on the scene and we carried her into Bonas Ratcliffe's butchers shop and they made that First Aid..."

2.Transcript of part of a recorded talk made in August 1987 by the Rev.Maurice Handford,Rector of Trinity Church,Buxton,who has since moved to Ireland. He was at home in Whitfield Villas, Low Leighton, when it was destroyed by a German bomb and Joan,his sister, killed.

"... I remember being in the house in the living room with my grandmother,she was in her 70s, and my sister was in the sitting room. She was playing the piano. I remember hearing a great noise and seeing this German aircraft only the height of the trees.I said to my grandmother 'my word,that's low !' and I made to go to the door and I never got there. There came a terrific thud and flash and I was out.How long I was out I don't know,it was some considerable time and what brought me to - the ARP [Air Raid Precautions] people were going through the debris and were pulling at me and they couldn't get me out because my foot was trapped under a beam and I think the pulling brought me round to consciousness... They got me out and my grandmother.She lived a year or so afterwards but it was too much. I was badly injured,it caught all the right side of my face for one thing,you can see the mark on my face...Dr Millward a local GP sewed it up... knocked my teeth out,my right eye was closed and they thought the sight had gone.It was closed for days but eventually it did open and I've had to wear specs ever since.It tore my ear down but that more or less mended up after a time... I was a nervous wreck,it certainly played hard with my nerves for long enough... however I was thankful I got out... They moved us to Ollersett View...and then on the Sunday to Woods Hospital in Glossop where I was in for about a week or so and she [grandmother] was in much longer... My father and mother were out at the time...My father was working late in Manchester because of the wartime,he worked on the railway,my mother was visiting friends at the Vine Tavern - not in the Tavern! ... my brother was at the ATC [Air Training Corps],they got a tremendous shock..."

3. Transcript of part of a recorded talk made in June 1987 by Mr John Duckworth of 2 Highfield Terrace. Mr Duckworth was the Son-in-Law of Mr Daniel McKellar and his daughter Brenda was a friend of Joan Handford.

"It was the evening of July 3rd 1942... talking to my wife we decided we would go to the pictures... As it happened Joan and Brenda came in together and we said... 'we're going to the pictures,would you like to come with us or do you want to stay with grandpa [Mr McKellar] ... the picture is Will Hay, we rather like him'...[Brenda] turns to Joan and says 'will you come to the pictures with us ?'... 'Oh',she says ' my daddy took me last night'... Brenda said 'Well,if I go with my mum and dad what will you be doing ?'. Joan said 'I'll be practising my piano'. 'And if I don't go what shall we do ?.' 'Play on the lawn'. Brenda pondered for a moment and said "I'll come with my mum and dad... so Joan went on then home..."

... we had a small allotment,very small one,at the top of Pingot Road as it is now,going down. Of course, it was a different area then,the ground sloped right down to the river – there's a river under those houses [Whitfield Villas]... and he [Mr McKellar] decided he'd take a book and read,sit reading,just there,so unfortunately he had gone there just at the wrong time..."

4. Transcript of part of a recorded talk made in July 1987 by the late Mr Wilfred Larkum who was New Mills Gas Engineer and Manager at the time of the air raid.

"... The bomb missed the gasworks... but he did machine-gun it... It would appear that machine-gun bullets had hit the large gasholder and it was in places on fire... what happened then I understand that Jack Slater and my brother took Albert Froggart by the ankles and he battered at the flames with a shovel and he managed luckily to get them out ... but the trouble was that they had managed to hit No 2 purifier with their bullets too and that was on fire... Well the fire brigade arrived... I've never seen so much foam and

One of the Junkers 88 (A4) aircraft which took part in the New Mills Air Raid. (Ron Collier).

Mr Daniel McKellar, Caretaker of the Methodist Chapel, who died from injuries, with his granddaughter Brenda. (Mr J. Duckworth).

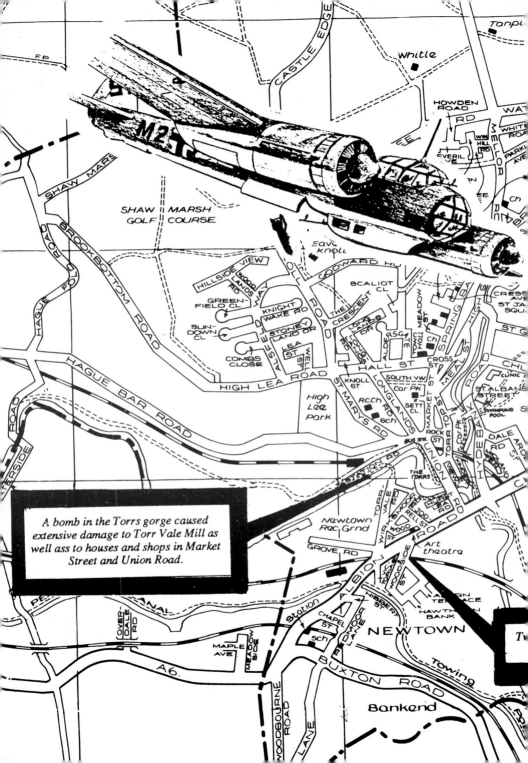

A bomb in the Torrs gorge caused extensive damage to Torr Vale Mill as well ass to houses and shops in Market Street and Union Road.

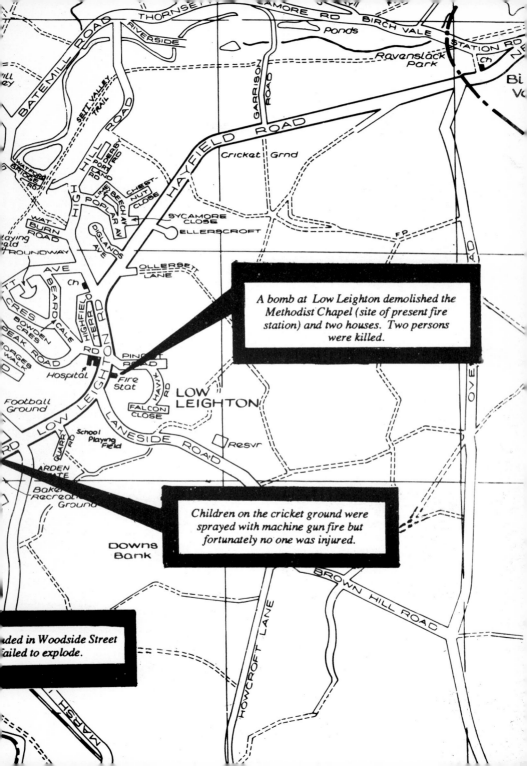

A bomb at Low Leighton demolished the Methodist Chapel (site of present fire station) and two houses. Two persons were killed.

Children on the cricket ground were sprayed with machine gun fire but fortunately no one was injured.

...ded in Woodside Street ...ailed to explode.

The "tin" Methodist Chapel at Low Leighton. (Mr M. Stores).

The demolished Methodist Chapel and Whitfield Villas at Low Leighton. (Rev. M. Handford).

water flying about but no way would the thing go out...
in the finish I decided to turn the thing off.This was
done with quite a bit of trepidation... thank God it
went out and didn't bang... It would appear that the
bomb that was let fly at the gasworks - the fin hit a
telegraph pole and took part of that away. I don't know
whether the fins didn't come off at that point but the
bomb continued on its way and landed in the river...

There's a sequel to the whole story really... next
morning... we decided to have a walk over and have a
look at where the bomb had dropped. Well,it would
appear that it was close to Lowe's Mill and the crowd
from that mill were getting the bomb out of the river
at the end of a rope. Well,they'd got the thing fast on
top of the railings and I just eased it off for them...
it would appear that the bomb had exploded but one
detonator hadn't and there was some powder left in
it...Anyway,we walked away and as we walked away who
should come along but the Chief Constable of Derby and
another officer.They caught this lot with this piece of
bomb in a barrow... they asked where they were taking
it.They were told 'the lock-up'... They collared this lot
with this bomb and the sum total of it was that they
gave my name in.I think the reason for that was the
fact that my father was Chairman of the Bench,perhaps
hoping it would help them...

The strange thing is that when the bombers came over...
one [bomb] came down on the junction of a road between
Woodside and Albion Road.It landed in the road and
split open and didn't explode.Another went through the
labour exchange building and I think that bed itself in
the railway embankment... Anyhow,this in the road hadn't
[exploded] and what happened then was that an Air Raid
Warden... he had been in the First World War and he
decided he was having none of this so he whipped the
detonators out. It seems he had dealt with such things
in the last war.He realised that if it was left to
officialdom they'd all be evacuated... so out came the
detonators and it finished with a policeman carting
them up to the lock-up in his pocket. They couldn't
handle the bomb as it was so they pulled all the TNT

out into buckets and threw it into the canal,and then
managed to get the bomb casing in the back of a Rolls
Royce that had been made into a truck... and they carted
that up to the lock-up..."

FATE OF THE AIRCRAFT

Ron Collier, the aviation historian who has specialised
in the study of aircraft crashes and other aircraft
incidents in the Peak District, has kindly provided
information about these two German aircraft.They appear
to have come from a base in France and flew up the
Irish Sea, turning inland at Southport. They continued
at a low level towards Stockport,circled the airfield at
Woodford and approached New Mills. With the hills in
front they dropped their bombs and machine gunned
indiscriminately. After leaving Hayfield,they continued
their flight eastwards over the Pennines and were
eventually shot down over Lincolnshire by four
Spitfires from a Polish Squadron based at Kirkland-in-
Lindsay. One crew of four was killed; the other crew
was taken prisoner. After the War, one member of this
crew sent Ron Collier a photograph of his aircraft
which had taken part in the raid. Mr Collier has kindly
provided a copy of the Air Ministry Reports of this
action, a letter from one of the Polish Pilots
describing the action in which he shot down one of the
aircraft,and copies of the Luftwaffe Reports recording
the loss of the two aircraft.

AIR MINISTRY REPORT

No 303/Polish/Squadron
Date: 3.7.42

20.05 Two aircraft scrambled - F/Sgt.Wunsche and
                                 F/Sgt.Popek.
                                 Yellow section
20.10 do.   - F/O Kolecki and
                                 Sgt.Rokitnicki
                                 White section

Yellow section first up were given course by operations
and F/Sgt.Wunsche observed two enemy aircraft,Ju.88s in

14

the area of Wragby,Lincs, which were flying very low in a south easterly direction.Sgt. Wunsche attacked first three quarters from astern and above firing a short burst from 300 yards. F/Sgt. Popek took the right hand aircraft and attacked from astern and above giving a long burst which he broke off at a distance of about 20 yards.The Ju. with both engines smoking was seen to hit farm buildings about 6 miles from Wragby.

F/Sgt.Wunsche and F/Sgt. Popek attacked the second Ju. 88 firing a series of short bursts.At this moment P/O Kolecki also attacked gave a burst and broke away, followed by Sgt. Rokitnicki who gave a series of bursts causing this Ju. 88 to force land near Harcastle. One blade of the propeller on F/Sgt. Popek's aircraft was damaged by bullet holes. Two Ju 88s destroyed.

REPORT BY MAJOR A ROKITNICKI, C.D.

3.7.1942 A very dull day turned into a very exciting experience. Yellow and White sections were at readiness at the dispersal point. Suddenly an announcement came over the speaker for the Yellow section to scramble-then seconds later the order for the White section to scramble also. The controller gave us several vectors to fly to intercept the Germans-then Yellow section excitedly reported sighting 2 JU 88 and engaged 1 in battle. Seconds later we spotted another JU 88 flying very low-tree height.Immediately my White section attacked the second JU 88-the section leader attacked and then peeled away giving me room to open fire and attack. When I had finished several bursts I could see the Ju 88s engine was on fire and a few seconds later the pilot of the plane made a forced landing on a small field.

The Bomber Air Crew scrambled from the JU 88 and started to run to the nearest bushes. I kept covering the German crew from the air until they were picked up by the Home Guard. May I say that they were an impressive and efficient group of soldiers.

A. Rokitnicki

RL 2 III / 761

Kdo.-St.	Luftflotte 3
Ausfertig.-Datum	5.7.42
Lfd.-Nr.	13
Datum	3.7.42
Einheit	K.Fl.Gr. 106 Kampf
Front od. Heimat	Front
Ort	Unbekannt
Ursache	Unbekannt
Flugzeug-muster	Ju 88 H 4
Werknr. u. Kennzeichen	140017 (M2 + KK)
Bruch %	100
Dienstst.-Grad Zu- u. Vorname Dienststellung	Hptm. Bergemann, Hans F Obgefr. Müller, Bernhard B Uffz. Fahning, Ernst Bf Uffz. Fickenwirth, Johannes Bs
Tote	/
Verletzte	/
Vermißt	4

Luftwaffe Report recording loss of one aircraft and crew

Kdo.-St.	Luftflotte 3
Ausfertig.-Datum	5.7.42
Lfd.-Nr.	14
Datum	3.7.42
Einheit	K.Fl.Gr.106 Kampf
Front od. Heimat	Front.
Ort	Unbekannt
Ursache	Unbekannt
Flugzeug-muster	Ju 88 A4
Werknr. u. Kennzeichen	140016 (M2+BK)
Bruch %	100
Dienstst.-Grad Zu- u. Vorname Dienststellung	Fw. Majer, Heinz F Obgfr. Wieberny, Horst B Obgfr. Schützschneider, Karl Bf Uffz. Frank, Theo Bs
Tote	Alle 4 am 13.8.42 für tot erklä
Verletzte	/
Vermld	4

Luftwaffe Report recording loss of one aircraft and death of one crew. (German military archives: Provided by Ron Collier)

APPENDIX

NEW MILLS TOWN COUNCIL: FILE CD/32:UNITS INVOLVED:

Wardens Posts BXI,BX2,BX3/4
Incident Post
Report Post
First Aid Posts(FAP) and Units(FAV)
Decontamination Depot(DD) which supplied Rescue Parties
RCB ?
Rest Centre (Welfare Centre ?)
Mobile Canteen
National Fire Service(NFS) at Low Leighton and the Swan
Reconstruction Panel
Ambulance
Police
PAP ?
Salvage Officer
Incident Medical Officer
Divisional   Controller(NW),Divisional   surveyor,County
Controller,Chairman of Supervisory Committee
Home Guard
Fire Guard Committee
Assistance Board-Out Station(Glossop)

NEW MILLS UDC FILE No CD/32 ENEMY
ACTION CORRESPONDENCE RE JULY 3rd.1942: REPORTS

1. R.Atkinson	Warden
	Wardens Post BXI
2. J.Flemming	Depot Superintendent
	First Aid Post BX
3. J W Marsland	Report Officer
	Report Post BX
4. (Unsigned)	Area Organiser
	Report Area 'B'
5. W Broadhurst	Deputy Chief Warden
6. W A Leigh	Air Raid Warden
	Wardens Post BX3/4
7. F.Bowmer	Depot Superintendent
	Decontamination Depot
8. E H Burditt	Chief Warden BX
9. J Walton	Incident Officer
10.J.Walton	Liaison Officer

CORRESPONDENCE

1. UDC notebook recording damage to property in the town
2. Letter from Mr Handford to UDC regarding claim for compensation,27 July 1942
3. UDC correspondence with the Lord Mayors National Air Raid Distress Fund regarding Mr Handford's claim for compensation,28 and 30 July,1,13,14,25 and 27 August 1942.
4. Letter from UDC to War Damage Commission regarding accounts for first aid repairs totalling £365.5.8, 13 August 1942
5. Letter from Mr Handford regarding unfinished clearance of bomb damage at the site of Whitfield Villas, 1 March 1943
6. UDC correspondence with Ministry of Pensions regarding the regulations for funeral grants for deaths arising from war operations,13,14, and 15 July 1942
7. UDC correspondence with Ministry of Health regarding alterations to Emergency Mortuary at Bate Mill , 13,20,21 July, and 14 and 28 September
8. Claims for and notes of damage to property from Mrs Travis,the Grove Paper Mill,the Brunswick Mill Dr Pemberton(owner of "Redgate"),Melias Ltd,E Potts, J Crossland
9. Letter to UDC from Electricity Commission acknowledging receipt of details of war damage to property of the Electricity Undertaking,7 October 1942
10. Particulars of damage to Electricity Department property at the Methodist Chapel and Whitfield Villas.
11. UDC correspondence with County Architect regarding repairs to Ollersett View Institution, 8 and 9 September 1942
12. Letter from County ARP Controller and copy of letter from Lord Trent with tributes for the work of the ARP Services during the raid.
13. Letter from Miss Bill, Westcliff-on-Sea and reply.

14 Letters of thanks to O/C 3rd Battalion Home
    Guard,Chapel-en-le-Frith (9 July 1942)Chairman
    ARP Supervising Committee, and Assistance
    Board-Out Station,Glossop
15 Letters of condolences from UDC to Mrs Duckworth
    and Mr and Mrs Travis,13 July 1942
16 Correspondence regarding the non-sounding of the
    air raid alarm on 3 July, 1942
17. Lists of articles salvaged from Whitfield Villas and
    the Methodist Chapel
18. Letter from UDC to Ministry of Health regarding
    total sum paid to contractors for repairs
    (£727.9.3), 14 December 1942
19. Other acknowledgements and notes

OFFICIAL FORMS

C.1 War Damage Commission for notification of damage to
property

F.P Leaflet No 1/42 Protection of Churches and similar
Buildings against Incendiary Attack

HM Office of Works List of Emergency Reserve of
Builders' Materials

Air Raid Precautions. Form for Identified Casualties

Ministry of Health. War Deaths. Emergency Mortuary and
Burial Arrangements.

Board of Trade.Form of Claim in Respect of War Damage
to Private Chattels.

Form for application for Injury Allowance

Copy of Circular 2112 Ministry of Health on Deaths due
to War Operations

Copy letter to UDC from Town Clerk regarding 'Distress
arising our of Air Raids", 3 October 1940.